CODE MONKEYS

Algorithms

BY JOHN WOOD

BookLife PUBLISHING

©2020
BookLife Publishing Ltd.
King's Lynn
Norfolk PE30 4LS

A catalogue record for this book is available from the British Library.

ISBN: 978-1-78637-976-4

Written by:
John Wood

Edited by:
Madeline Tyler

Designed by:
Danielle Webster-Jones

All facts, statistics, web addresses and URLs in this book were verified as valid and accurate at time of writing.

No responsibility for any changes to external websites or references can be accepted by either the author or publisher.

Contents

Words that look like **this** can be found in the glossary on page 24.

Welcome
TO THE JUNGLE

A code monkey is a curious, clever little thing. It wants to know all about computers and coding. Let's follow the code monkeys and learn about coding too!

A code monkey can also be very annoying. Plug that back in!

FIRST THINGS FIRST

 **COMPUTER =** a machine that can carry out <u>instructions</u>

 **CODING =** writing a set of instructions, called code, to tell computers what to do

 **PROGRAMMER =** a person who writes code (like a human code monkey)

 Computers are everywhere. Desktops, laptops, smartphones and tablets are all computers. There are even computers in surprising places, from fridges to lampposts.

Coding
IN THE WILD

The internet is built out of code. All the games, videos and websites you can find on the internet were made by clever programmers.

Maybe one day you could build a website yourself. However, first you need to learn how to talk to computers in a language they understand. This is called a programming language, or code.

CHIMPTUBE

If you could make a website, what would you put on it?

7

WHAT IS AN Algorithm?

An algorithm is a set of instructions. Think of an algorithm like a set of steps that have been carefully written. They tell someone or something exactly what to do.

Algorithms are designed to solve problems. They solve problems such as 'how will the computer count the score in this game' or 'how will somebody be able to search for videos on this website'.

The algorithms that the websites YouTube and Google use are very <u>complicated</u>.

STUPID CoMPUTerS

Computers are very good at certain things, such as adding up numbers, or doing the same thing over and over again. Computers don't get tired or read the code wrong.

Search

LOADING...

However, computers cannot work things out or come up with ideas on their own. They have to be given simple instructions to follow.

If there is something wrong with an algorithm, computers will break or do the wrong thing.

Flow Charts

Flow charts are a great way of seeing how a computer follows instructions. Look at the algorithm on the next page. It has to be very **detailed** to make sure the computer does everything right.

Meet our latest creation — Chimpandroid. He will carry out our algorithms.

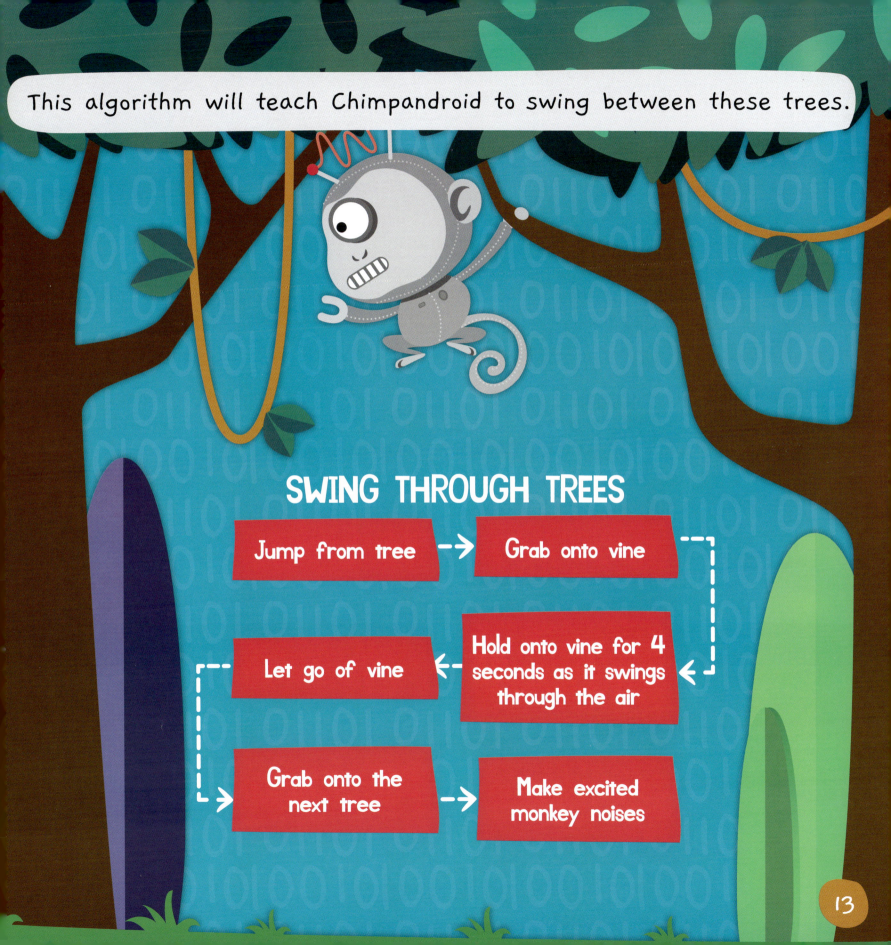

This algorithm will teach Chimpandroid to swing between these trees.

SWING THROUGH TREES

Jump from tree → Grab onto vine

Hold onto vine for 4 seconds as it swings through the air

Let go of vine ←

Grab onto the next tree → Make excited monkey noises

13

Programs

Programs are made up of lots of algorithms. A program is a piece of code that can be 'run' by a computer.

'Run' just means that the computer goes through all the algorithms and does what it is told.

A program is written in a programming language. There are lots of different programming languages. A program also needs a **device** to run on.

A game on your PC is a program. An internet browser is a program, too.

Algorithms
IN THE REAL WORLD

Algorithms do lots of complicated things in the real world.

Algorithms control the programs that help artists create **animated** films.

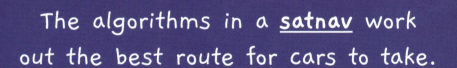

The algorithms in a **satnav** work out the best route for cars to take.

Algorithms **compress** sounds and videos. This lets you talk to people across the world on video calls.

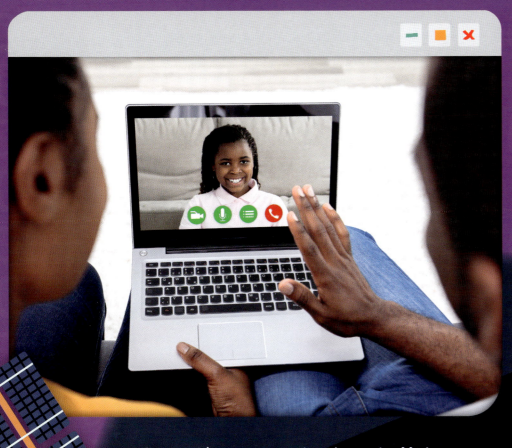

Algorithms control **satellites** that are up in space.

Algorithms work out how to give you the best results when you search for something on the internet.

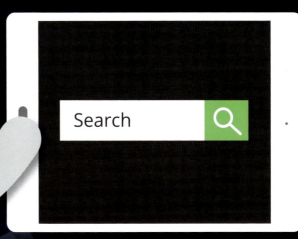

Search

BLOCKS OF Code

Algorithms can be sorted into a little chunk of code. This chunk of code is given a name, and it can be used again in different parts of the code.

Many languages, such as Python or JavaScript, call these chunks 'functions'. Scratch calls these chunks 'blocks'.

define   Monkey Business

For example, instead of making an algorithm every time you want Chimpandroid to pick his nose, you could create a chunk of code called nosePick.

nosePick

Put finger up nose
Move finger around to collect bogey
Take finger out of nose
Roll bogey
Flick bogey

Now, every time you want Chimpandroid to pick his nose, you can just tell the computer to run the nosePick function, or block.

Monkey See

Let's look at how an algorithm looks in real code. This is Scratch.

WHEN IT IS RAINING

Say 'It's raining!'
Move into the tree for shelter
Sit down

```
when 🏳 clicked

say  It's raining!  for  2  seconds

glide  3  secs to  Tree1 ▾

switch costume to  Monkey Sitting ▾
```

Here is a function in Python. It makes Chimpandroid guess a number, wait for one second, and then roll a dice. If Chimpandroid is right, he says 'I win!'. Otherwise it loops back to the start.

```python
from random import import randint
from time import sleep, time

def monkeyRoll():
    guess = str(randint(1,6))
    print('I pick the number ' + guess)
    sleep(1)
    dice = str(randint(1,6))
    print('Rolling dice... it\'s a ' + dice)
    if guess == dice:
        print('I win!')
    else:
        print('Oh dear. I\'ll try again.')
        monkeyRoll()

monkeyRoll()
```

You can see the different steps of the algorithm highlighted in different colours. By the way, sleep means wait!

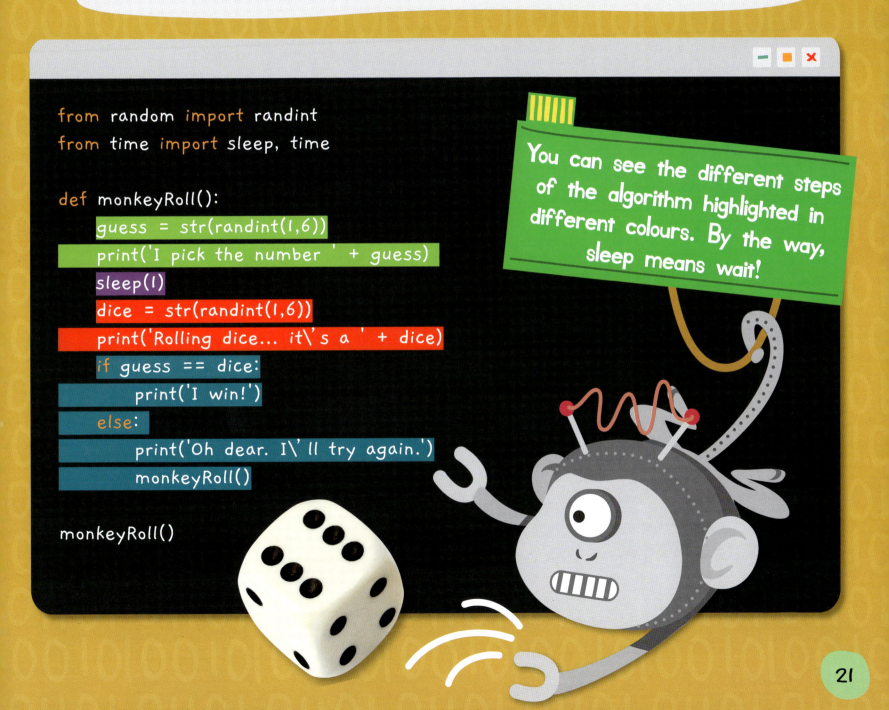

Monkey Do

It is time to build your own algorithm. The younger code monkeys need some milk. Write an algorithm for getting milk from the fridge and pouring it into a cup, ready for the code monkeys to drink.

To test your algorithm, try reading it to a friend. Your friend must do exactly as the algorithm says, and nothing else. Did your friend get a cup of milk ready for the code monkeys?

Turn this page upside down for an idea of what this algorithm might look like.

Answers
Go to fridge
Open fridge door
Take the bottle of milk out
Close fridge door
Take the top off the bottle of milk
Grab a cup
Pour milk into cup
Stop pouring when the cup is full
Put top back on milk bottle
Open fridge door
Put milk back
Close fridge door

Glossary

animated	when lots of images are put together to make it look like something is moving
complicated	made of many different parts and therefore hard to understand
compress	(in computers) make a file smaller so it takes up less space on a computer and is easier to transfer over the internet
detailed	full of facts and information, and not leaving anything important out
device	a machine or invention made to do something
instructions	a set of steps that explain how something is done
JavaScript	a type of programming language that is good for building websites
Python	a type of programming language that is made to be easy to use
satellites	machines in space that travel around planets, take photographs and collect and send information
satnav	a device that uses satellite signals to find the best route for a car to follow
Scratch	a type of programming language made up of pictures and words – good for learning how to code

Index